231

That Lawsuit Against the Bible

That Lawsuit Against the Bible

by

HARRY RIMMER, Sc.D., D.D.

TENTH EDITION

WM. B. EERDMANS PUBLISHING COMPANY

Grand Rapids   Michigan

THAT LAWSUIT AGAINST THE BIBLE
By HARRY RIMMER, Sc.D., D.D.

PRINTED IN THE UNITED STATES OF AMERICA

CONTENTS

That Lawsuit Against the Bible

1.

"TOO MANY QUAIL"

ONE of the most interesting cases to appear upon the calendar of any court in the United States has recently been concluded in the Fourth District Municipal Court of New York City. This case is officially known as "William Floyd vs. Harry Rimmer," but it would be more accurate to call it "Infidelity vs. The Word of God." On one side of the issue the weight of a great group, composed of Atheists, Free Thinkers, Modernists, Humanists, and Liberal Jews was directed to the task of discrediting the Bible and proving that it was not and could not be the inspired Word of God. On the other side of the issue a group of simple, believing Christians stood steadfast for the infallibility of the Book, and saw their confidence justified in as complete a victory as has ever been recorded.

Modernists have long professed to desire a "day in court," and in this trial that day was granted them. But when their conclusions and teachings were subjected to the rigid demands of the law of evidence, and *proof* for their statements and theories was demanded, they found it utterly impossible to establish a case against the historic view of the Bible. This book is a statement of the issues involved, and

the record of the trial which ended in legally establishing the position of all who hold that the Word
of God is inerrant.

Many men have died for believing the Bible, and
countless others have languished in dungeons for
their faith in this Book. But so far as I know, I am
the only man who has ever been sued for damages
for believing and teaching the perfection of the
Sacred Text! And I have had that strange experience
twice in the last ten years.

The genesis of this present case is rooted in the
past. For fifteen years the Research Science Bureau,
a corporation of which I am the president, had been
broadcasting an offer of one hundred dollars to any
person who would establish a scientific mistake in
the Bible. This offer was published in the newspapers and magazines of twenty-seven different coun-
tries. It was publicised in platform meetings all over
America, and was often repeated on the radio. In the
fifteen years during which this offer was in effect
there was an enormous volume of correspondence
concerning it, as the reader may well imagine. Every fantastic theory and wild imagining of unbelief
was addressed to the committee which decided the
contest, and some weird letters were received. Every question from the capacity of Noah's ark to the
suggestion that apples would not grow in the climate
of Eden was handled by this committee in that
period of fifteen years, with the result that no person was able in that span of time to establish a case
of error in the Bible.

With one exception, every contender withdrew
his demand when the answer of the committee had

been received. To my mind, this is one of the greatest testimonies to the infallibility of the Bible we have ever seen. Thousands of communications were received by the Research Bureau, from men and women in walks of life which varied from day laborers to college presidents. Yet the most skeptical inquirer seemed to be satisfied with the reply furnished, and conceded that the mistake was his, and should not be charged against the Word. We have often thought that a series of articles concerning these questions and our answers would be of great interest to the Christian public. If ever we do write such a series, we feel that we could properly name the series "The Philosophy of Ignorance" because of the fact that every question submitted sprang from ignorance of the text of the Bible, or from ignorance of the science involved. And the less a person seemed to know about either subject, the more certain he appeared to be that science and Scripture could not be harmonized.

The one exception mentioned above occurred in 1929. A man in California, who claimed to be a retired Colonel of the Quarter-master's Corps in the United States Army, submitted a strange thesis consisting of four typewritten pages of matter. Reduced to a simple statement, the Colonel contended that the record of the quail that fed hungry Israel during the wilderness journey, constituted a mathematical mistake in the Bible. On the ground that mathematics is a science, he demanded the award.

He made out his case as follows: there were about two and a half million people in the Exodus, and when they made camp it would require 144 square miles to accommodate them. According to his view, the Bible states that quail were sent by the Lord to feed this group, and that the quail covered the ground all around camp to the extent of a day's journey in every direction, and to a solid depth of two cubits. The Colonel contended that a "day's journey" was 28 miles, and since the quail covered the ground on all four sides of the camp, there were 4,569 square miles of quail piled up 44 inches deep on the surface of the earth! Parenthetically, it should be remembered that all these figures are from the Colonel's brief. Deducting from this area the 144 square miles of the camp, we have left 4,425 square miles of quail. The Colonel then assured us that he knew from experience that 64 quail could be counted in each cubic foot, and then proceeded to figure the cubic area of the mass of quail. He came out of this mental huddle with the positive statement that there were twenty-nine trillion, six hundred thirteen billion, nine hundred ninety-one million, two hundred sixty thousand, one hundred and seventy-one quail in the pile. Then he divided this number by the two and a half million people in the company, and found that every Jew had to eat twelve million, two hundred sixty-six thousand, one hundred seventy-one quail to get rid of the ration which he insisted had been sent them. To this was added the difficulty that every member of the Horde would have to pick and carry to camp, ninety-seven birds per second for thirty-six hours. This, he concluded, was a scientific impossibility, and he demanded the reward on the ground that he had thus "proved" a scientific error in the Bible.

Frankly, when the committee received this amazing opus, we thought somebody was playing a practical joke on us. But on the assumption that the correspondent might really be serious, we returned an answer. We pointed out that the "day's journey" of the wandering was never twenty-eight miles, but nearer an average of three miles. We showed him that the quail were on only two sides of the camp, so that he did not have a square to figure from. Then we pointed out that the quail were flying low, two cubits high *above* the face of the earth, and had to be netted or knocked down by the hunters. All of which changed the alleged factors of his calculations so completely as to destroy his case.

Instead of accepting the answer of the committee, the Colonel brought suit against me for the hundred dollars. The suit was tried in New York, through an attorney named Wheless, and came into court twice. My attorney was an eminent Christian, Mr. James E. Bennet, who is well known to many who love the Lord Jesus.

The first time the case came on the calendar, my attorney made the plea that suit had been improperly made against me as an individual, whereas it was the corporation which had made the offer. The case was dismissed without prejudice, which allowed the plaintiff to bring it back into court later. The second time the plaintiff's attorney evidently had secured the services of a lawyer to help him get his papers in order, and this time the case was decided on the issue involved; namely, "Had the plaintiff proved an error in the Bible? If so, had an offer

been made which had not been paid, thus consti-
tuting a breach of contract?"

The court decided that no error had been proved,
and that no award had been made or was due. The
judge seemed to think that as the plaintiff, Colonel
Nichols, was *not* there when the episode happened,
he made a poor witness as to the fact involved. But
as Moses *was* there and did see the event, the judge
decided to take his word as to what transpired.

So after fifteen years, we had a legally flawless
record, and were much encouraged in our belief
that the Bible, while not a text-book of science, is
still the inspired Word of God, and that regardless
of the issue involved God knew the facts. Therefore His Word must be as infallible on scientific
subjects as it is on matters of history or morals. With
this perfect record, and at the suggestion of one of
the Directors of the Corporation, in 1939 we withdrew and cancelled the original offer of one hundred
dollars for the discovery of such an error.

Instead, the Corporation offered and does now
offer, THE SUM OF ONE THOUSAND DOL-
LARS to the person and/or persons who shall dis-
cover and prove an error of science in the Bible.
This offer is made subject to the following five
conditions:

1. All applicants must state their case in writing, five
   duplicate typewritten copies of each thesis being submitted, in order that each member of the Committee on award may have an identical copy for consideration.

2. Each thesis must be accompanied by the proof and
   evidence of the error which is alleged to be in the
   Sacred Text.

3. The Committee shall not be obligated to attempt to harmonize scientific theories with interpretations of the Text, but will deal only with cases where an established fact of science is contradicted by a plain and clear statement in the Bible. In all cases the decision shall be determined by the accepted Hebrew text of the Old Testament, and the accepted Greek text of the New Testament.

4. The Committee shall meet once each quarter, and shall then answer all applicants who may have submitted a claim during the preceding three months.

5. The decision of a majority of the Committee shall be final in all cases.

This offer was read from the pulpit of The Central Baptist Church in New York City, and the conditions were specifically set forth. A member of the church, who attended the meeting, desired to give some publicity to the meetings, and the following day he inserted in the New York *Herald-Tribune* an advertisement, stating, "Dr. Harry Rimmer, speaking nightly at the Central Baptist Church, will pay $1,000.00 for a scientific error in the Bible." This ad was inserted without my knowledge or consent, and paid for entirely by this one member. Two days later I received a letter from one William Floyd, stating that he had read this ad, and was submitting five "scientific mistakes" in the Bible and demanding the thousand dollars. The letter was a personal communication addressed to me as an individual, so I laid it aside with my other mail intending to send him one of the printed announcements containing the address of the Committee. But a couple of days following, I received a legal summons and complaint, stating that Mr. Floyd had brought

suit against me for the sum offered by the Corporation, and by the strangest coincidence, the same
lawyer who had met defeat ten years before was the
attorney for Mr. Floyd. And by an even odder co-
incidence, the brief was the same as the one filed by
Colonel Nichols ten years ago!

I have seldom seen such excitement as the daily
press displayed over this matter! There were head-
lines in every paper in the country which subscribes
to the Associated Press service: one New York paper
published a two-page "spread" in its Sunday edition,
and the Radio News sent transcriptions out to its
multiplied scores of station-customers. News magazines, such as *Newsweek* ran columns on the issue,
and the Bible got more publicity than could have
been purchased with millions of dollars. Every so
often the Enemy does over-reach himself, and helps
to call attention to the Word of Life. Correspondence swept over us from every state in the Union,
asking for information and news of the approaching
trial.

This present book is an answer in a permanent
form, to those many requests. We will state the
specific charges against the Bible, as they are set forth
in the suit, and shall then present our answer to each
one in turn. From this we will pass on to the additional fifty-one charges against the scientific accuracy of the Scripture, all filed by this plaintiff and
his attorney. From that we will press on to the story
of the trial. When the case finally came on the calendar and was heard by the judge assigned, the papers
in the case had mounted up to an impressive amount.
The brains and ability of the Free (?) Thinking (?)

world were assembled to crush the Bible once and for all, and the Court gave them every possible advantage. All of which makes the resultant complete victory for the Bible the more remarkable. It seems that God is still able to sustain His Word, and that there is wisdom in depending upon it for our present comfort and future destiny.

To set this matter before the reader in an orderly fashion, we will present each of the arguments against the Bible by itself, and then give the refutation, pointing out the error involved.

2

THE FIRST ARGUMENT

UNDER the laws of the State of New York, the
plaintiff in a legal action may demand the
privilege of examining the defendant before the
trial, in an attempt to establish certain facts which
may help his case. In this action, it was stipulated
that such an examination before trial should be
conducted, but that it should be limited to matters
which were germane and material to the question.
Accordingly, I met the attorney, MR. WHELESS,
in the office of MR. JAMES BENNET, who so capa-
bly handled the case for the defense, and there submitted to such an examination.

The stenographer who accompanied MR.
WHELESS had been engaged for the occasion from
a bureau that supplies stenographic help, and after
the examination we had a friendly conversation. She
informed me that in seeking a stenographer, MR.
WHELESS had requested that an atheist be sent
to handle the examination. Somewhat bewildered
by this strange request, the office manager replied,
"Mister, we deal in stenographic help, not in assorted
religions! If you want a stenographer we can supply
one, but if it is religion you are interested in, call
up the Y.M.C.A."! Thereupon, being a somewhat

perverse man, he asked this young lady if she was a Christian. Upon her assurance that she was, he assigned her to the case.

When the examination began, MR. WHELESS ignored the agreement, and sought to introduce into the record matters that were in no way connected with the original complaint, and to uncover material which he apparently hoped would be useful in some later action. I have the copy of this examination before me as I write, and it begins with these words: "EXAMINATION BEFORE TRIAL of the Defendant Harry Rimmer, taken pursuant to stipulations entered into in the above entitled action between the parties thereto . . . " Time after time MR. BENNET reminded MR. WHELESS of this agreement, but the attorney for the plaintiff utterly ignored the warnings. Violating the stipulation repeatedly, he sought to obtain information which was utterly outside the issues. In the entire examination, MR. WHELESS asked a total of sixty-one questions, and thirty-four times MR. BENNET objected and instructed the defendant not to answer.

But in the very small part of the examination when MR. WHELESS kept within the bounds of the agreement, it was established beyond any question that I had not authorized the advertisement that was the basis of the suit, and was in total ignorance of its insertion in the newspaper. To establish this point, we here offer this one portion of the record of the examination:

Q. Now, the subject of your lectures made in New York several weeks ago in a Central Baptist Church was "The Harmony of Science and the Scriptures," was it not? A. Yes, that is right; that was one of the general themes for the week.

Q. How frequently did you speak there at the Central Baptist Church? A. Eight days, to be exact.

Q. Was any announcement made in the newspapers in New York City on that series of lectures?

MR. BENNET: I object to that; you should ask him whether he made any announcement.

MR. WHELESS: I did not ask him who made the announcement; I asked him if there was an announcement made.

DR. RIMMER: I cannot answer that; no announcement was made by me.

Q. I ask you whether an announcement was made in the *Herald-Tribune* on the 31st day of October, 1939—? A. I cannot answer that; I never saw the *Herald-Tribune* on that day; I never knew, or heard, or had been advised that such an ad had been inserted until I was served with the papers in this action.

Q. Now, I show you a copy of the *Herald-Tribune*, dated October 31, 1939. On page 2, under the heading "Public Notices," there appears an announcement relating to yourself and your lectures at the Central Baptist Church which reads as follows:

> "Rev. Dr. Harry Rimmer speaks nightly this week and Sunday at Central Baptist Church, 92nd Street and Amsterdam Avenue on 'Harmony of Science and Scripture.' He offers one thousand dollars for a scientific error in the Bible. Public invited. 7:45."

Is that the announcement that was made in the *Herald-Tribune?* A. May I see it; I have not seen it yet; this is the first time I ever saw it in print.

Q. But it is correctly quoted? A. That is, you read it as it is in the *Herald-Tribune.*

(Paper accepted into the record and marked Plaintiff's Exhibit I for identification).

Q. You say you never before saw that announcement and knew nothing about it except by hearsay? A. That is right.

Q. What hearsay? A. The incorporation of that ad in the complaint served upon me.

Q. That is not hearsay.

MR. BENNET: Yes, it is.

Q. Did you never hear it mentioned before? A. Not before the time I read it in the complaint.

Q. Was any other announcement of your recent series of lectures in this city made in any newspaper? A. I cannot answer that yes or no, because I do not customarily read the ads in the announcements; but I did authorize one to be made.

Q. When was that? A. The Monday that the meeting started. I cannot recall the date—Oh, yes, the date was October 30th. I authorized Mr. Morris Townsend, who is the official publicity director for Central Baptist Church to insert the following, which he addressed by telegram to the City Editor of the *Herald-Tribune*:

"Doctor Harry Rimmer, President Research Science Bureau, speaking each night this week at Central Baptist Church, 92 Street and Amsterdam Avenue, offers one thousand dollars to discoverer of scientific error in the Bible. Conditions stated nightly. Investigate.

(Signed) Morris M. Townsend."

Such a copy was sent to the *New York Sun, New York Times, New York World-Telegram, New York*

Journal American and the *Herald-Tribune* of New York.

(Copy of telegram marked Plaintiff's Exhibit 2 for Identification).

Q. I notice, Dr. Rimmer, that the text of your telegraphic instructions to the newspapers in respect to your lectures in New York, differs somewhat from the text of the announcement as published in the *Herald Tribune* — Plaintiff's Exhibit 1 for Indentification. Can you explain how or why that difference in text occurred? A. I had nothing to do with that publication to which you refer in the *Herald Tribune* of the 31st day of October, 1939. The telegrams were sent as news items by Morris Townsend, for attention of the City Editors, and were not advertisements. At no time did I insert, or authorize the insertion in any New York publication of a paid advertisement concerning this offer.

Q. Do you know whether this announcement of October 31st was paid for? A. I do not know.

Q. That was sent by the publicity agent of the Central Baptist Church? A. It was not. Your Exhibit 2, which I read to you, is a copy of a form sent to the City Editors of the New York papers to attract attention to a story which we thought would make a good news item.

Q. So the text of the telegram to the *Herald Tribune* is the same as that of the telegrams to the other newspapers? A. The text of the telegram that was sent to the City Editor of the *Herald Tribune* is the same as that sent to the other editors.

Q. Do you know who paid for these telegrams? A. I cannot answer that, no.

Q. Or, who paid for the insertion of the text of it in the public notices of the *Herald Tribune?* A. As far as I know, this telegram was never published in the public notices of the *Herald Tribune* and was never offered as a paid advertisement.

Q. Now, how did Mr. Townsend, the publicity man, get this information contained in these telegrams? A. I gave it to him personally over the telephone, and he read it back to me to be sure the text was accurate.

Q. Then the text was the accurate statement as made to Mr. Townsend over the telephone, and you approved it? A. That is right.

Q. So the text referred to correctly represents your statement to Mr. Townsend? A. If you mean the text of the telegram, yes.

Q. In connection with your public discussions of the general topic on Harmony between Science and the Scriptures, have you written and published any of your lectures in books or pamphlets on the subject? A. Yes, I have published both books and pamphlets on this subject.

MR. WHELESS: Mr. Bennet stated to me the other day over the telephone that the offer made at the lectures of Dr. Rimmer, the defendant, was in accordance with the statement made in the answer of the defendant Rimmer, and was the same offer which was made in lectures whenever any offer of any kind was made. He has produced the original copy of that upon this hearing, which offer he has here ready to produce.

3

THE COMPLAINT

AT THIS point a certified copy of the offer of the Bureau was handed to MR. WHELESS and incorporated into the record, so there was no chance that he could be ignorant of the fact that no contract existed between his client and the defendant. The Complaint alleged that five specific scientific errors existed in the Bible, and that the citation thereof constituted a contract between HARRY RIMMER and any person who answered the ad which had appeared in the New York *Herald-Tribune*. But the examination before trial clearly established the fact that the defendant did not publish the said ad, that he had not authorized it, and that he had no knowledge of its appearance until after suit was filed against him on the basis of this ad.

If the reader should wonder that a lawyer would still proceed to trial on a basis of a "breach-of-contract" where no semblance of a contract existed, he needs only to remember that we are dealing here with men who parade their infidelity, and who seek any occasion to vaunt themselves against the Bible. When men deny the very existence of God, they are not amenable to rules in any other lesser sphere.

The attorney for the plaintiff explained the co-incidence between the two suits of 1929 and 1939 by stating that both plaintiffs in the different actions took their data from a book which he had written, "IS IT GOD'S WORD?" We glanced through this book, and found it to be a re-hash of all the errors and blindness of the late Col. Robert Ingersoll. The very title of the book, "Is It God's Word?" is a plagiarism; as this is just the same question the Devil asked in the Garden of Eden! Thus the original letter of the plaintiff, MR. FLOYD, was NOT original, it was just five excerpts from his attorney's book, which in turn was a poorly compiled summary of the second-hand vaporings of infidels for many generations past. It would be most unkind to reproduce this letter photostatically, as it is worse than messy.

The same criticism applies to the papers and subpoenas drawn up by the attorney for the plaintiff. The original subpoena served on me commands my appearance before an un-named and unknown judge, at nine o'clock of the morning of a date not given, on a day not mentioned in the subpoena! I do not know much law, but I do know that the first requirement of a subpoena is that it must state the time and the place! Yet here is a man who states that he has practiced law for fifty years, and he still cannot fill out a simple legal document in clear and lucid style. He represents a man who cannot write a clear and neat letter, and between them they want to tell Moses how he should have written the Pentateuch!

As we shall refer frequently to the original complaint, we reproduce it here, that the reader may be familiar with its weird and grotesque claims.

MUNICIPAL COURT: CITY OF NEW YORK
BOROUGH OF MANHATTAN: FOURTH DISTRICT

WILLIAM FLOYD,
    Plaintiff,

 —against—

(Rev.) HARRY RIMMER and
CENTRAL BAPTIST CHURCH OF
NEW YORK, a Corporation,
    Defendants.

COMPLAINT

The plaintiff above named, by Joseph Wheless his attorney, for his cause of action against the above named defendant, says:

First. Plaintiff is a citizen and resident of the State and City of New York, residing at No. 114 East 31st Street, Manhattan; the defendant Rimmer is an itinerant preacher or evangelist resident of the City of Los Angeles, California, traveling about the country as a "Fundamentalist" Christian preacher: the defendant Central Baptist Church of New York, is a corporation under the Religious Corporation Law, with its principal place of business at 92nd Street and Amsterdam Avenue, in the Borough of Manhattan, City of New York, the defendant Rimmer being at present residing in this City at the Hotel Wellington, Seventh Avenue and 55th St.

Second. That the defendants printed and published, each with the knowledge and consent of the other, and as joint and several promisors, on October 31st, 1939, in the newspaper *The Herald Tribune* in the City of New York, a certain public advertisement and offer of contract, addressed to all persons, under the heading "Public Notices," in terms as follows:

> "Rev. Dr. Harry Rimmer speaks nightly this week and Sunday at Central Baptist Church, 92nd Street and Amsterdam Avenue, on 'Harmony of Science and Scripture.' He offers one thousand dollars for a scientific error in the Bible. 7:45."

Third. That on November 1, 1939, plaintiff having read the said advertised offer of contract, accepted the same in writing by registered letter addressed to the defendant Rimmer in care of and at the above stated address of the defendant Central Baptist Church of New York, and complied with and fully performed its terms and conditions by citing and presenting to him several scientific errors that appear in the said Bible, as below specified, whereby a valid and binding contract was concluded and entered into between plaintiff and said defendants, in accordance with which plaintiff demanded payment to him of said offered award of one thousand dollars, and in view of the indicated fact that the defendant Rimmer was transiently in the City and would leave the City on or about November 5, 1939, requested reply at once: which letter and request said defendant ignored and did not reply: and defendants did not pay or intend to pay the said reward.

Fourth. That the scientific errors in the Bible which the plaintiff specified and pointed out to defendant Rimmer in said letter of acceptance of his offer for a scientific error in the Bible, were in substance and effect the following, to wit:

a). That the Bible states that the Creation was effected in six (6) days, whereas the universe has evolved gradually through millions of years; as proven by many branches of science;

b). That according to the first chapter of Genesis the beasts were created before man, but according to the second chapter after man; neither occurred as there erroneously stated;

c). That according to Genesis, chapter vi, 19-22, Noah took two (2) of every kind of living thing into the ark, whereas in chapter vii, 2-5, he took into said ark "by sevens, the male and his female," which allegations are not scientifically true, and said ark, as described in chapter vi, 14-16, could not possibly contain all such animals and living things and the food necessary for them during the long voyage;

d). That according to Leviticus xi, 4-6, it is stated that the camel does not divide the hoof and that the coney and the hare chew the cud, none of which statements is scientifically true, but the contrary is in each instance true;

e). That in the Book of Exodus of said Bible, chapter 16, verse 13, it is stated:

"And it came to pass, that at even the quails came up, and covered the camp;" which said bare statement is elaborated and detailed specifications given, in Numbers xi, 31-33:

"31. And there went forth a wind from the Lord, and brought quails from the sea, and let them fall by the camp, as it were a day's journey on this side, and as it were a day's journey on the other side, round about the camp, and as it were two cubits high upon the face of the earth.

"32.   And the people stood up all day, and all that night, and all the next day, and they gathered up the quails: he that gathered least gathered ten homers — (the *homer* equals approximately 80 gallons) : and they spread them all abroad for themselves round about the camp.

"33.   And while the flesh was yet between their teeth, ere it was chewed, the wrath of the Lord was kindled against the people, and the Lord smote the people with a very great plague" — (probably a sort of divine botulism or ptomaine poisoning, which according to verse 34 murdered the great numbers of the expectant eaters, thus vitiating the divine promise of verses 19-20, that, to wit:

"19.   Ye shall not eat one day, nor two days, nor five days, neither ten days nor twenty days:

"20.   But even a whole month, until it come out at your nostrils, and it be loathsome unto you.")

Fifth. Upon information and belief, and according to the generally accepted exegetic definitions and explanations and accredited Biblical scholarship no doubt well known to the clerical defendants, and formerly submitted in detail to the defendant the Rev. Rimmer by another claimant of a reward offered by him for proof of "scientific error in the Bible," the following facts and the simple application of the science of mathematics to the data supplied by above quoted verses from the Book of Numbers and related texts, completely demonstrate that said Quail Story of the Bible is scientifically and factually untrue and impossible to be true, to wit:

a).   That a biblical "day's journey" as mentioned in said texts, is approximately twenty-eight (28) miles;

b). That a deposition of quails surrounding the camp on all sides for a day's journey all about, would be a solid mass of quails measuring fifty-six (56) miles in every direction around the camp, or 3136 square miles of quails, less the area of the central camp;

c). That the said camp of the Hebrews as used during their traditional wanderings in the wilderness, was twelve (12) miles square, or 144 square miles in extent, which area being deducted from the 3136 square miles above stated, leaves 2992 square miles of quails covering the face of the earth round about the camp, piled up two cubits high;

d). That a biblical cubit, as used in said texts, is approximately 22 inches; two cubits would be 44 inches, or 3.66 feet, to which height said quails are alleged to have been piled up in an area of 2992 square miles—an extent equal to the combined areas of the States of Delaware and Rhode Island;

e). That one mile contains 5280 linear feet; one square mile contains 27,878,400 square feet; in 2992 square miles there are a total of 83,412,172,800 square feet, said to have been covered with quails piled 3.66 feet high above the camp.

f). That the cubical contents of this mass of quails would be approximately 305,288,552,448 cubic feet of quails; estimating that each quail, pressed in the mass, would occupy about 3x3 inches of space, allows some 27 cubic inches of space per quail in the pile. One cubic foot contains 1728 cubic inches; with 27 cubic inches per quail, one cubic foot would contain 64 quails. The total number of quails, therefore, in this mass or mess of quails would be 19,538,467,356,672 quails presented to the eye or mind of Fundamentalist Faith;

g). That according to verse 21 of said chapter xi, there were in round biblical numbers 600,000 foot-men or armed soldiers in the camp, or according to more formal census returns taken and reported about that time (Num. 1, 45-46), there were 603,550 men from 20 years old upwards fit for soldiering; allowing these warriors to be but one in four of the entire number, with old men, women, children, the 22,000 levites, camp-followers, slaves, etc. there would be a minimum of some 2,414,200 Chosen People in the camp; on which basis there would be a per capita of 8,093,144 quails;

h). That the people stood for 36 hours (xi,32) gathering in the quails; this would require each person to garner an average of 299,129 quails per hour, or 4985 quails per minute, or 85 quails per second, without time for rest or for the time of walking back and forth an average of thirty-odd miles to and from the camp with each load of quails gathered, or for somehow stowing the 2992 square miles of quails in the 144 square-mile camp, already full of tents, people and cattle, besides many other obvious impossibilities implied in the sacred texts cited, —

all disproving the truth and good faith of defendants' claim that the said Bible contains no "scientific error" or errors against scientific truth and fact, as above demonstrated by these few examples out of very many which the defendants must know, if they know anything about their Bible and about the truths of science.

WHEREFORE Plaintiff demands judgment against defendants in the sum of One Thousand ($1,000.00) Dollars reward offered with interest from November 1, 1939, and costs and disbursements of suit.

(Signed) Joseph Wheless
          Joseph Wheless
          Attorney for Plaintiff,
10 East 40th Street,
Manhattan, New York City

STATE OF NEW YORK \] ss.
NEW YORK COUNTY

WILLIAM FLOYD, being duly sworn, deposes and says: That he is the plaintiff in the within action; that he has read the foregoing Complaint and knows the contents thereof and that the same is true to his own knowledge, except as to the matters therein stated to be alleged on information and belief, and that as to those matters he believes it to be true.

> (Signed) William Floyd
> William Floyd

SWORN TO and Subscribed before me this 4th day of November, 1939.

(Signed) Esther Ruth Saks, Notary Public, N. Y. Co. Clerk No. 17, Reg. No. 1931. Commission expires March 30, 1941.

4

DEFENDANT'S REPLY

My reply to this Complaint was duly filed, in the following form:

MUNICIPAL COURT: CITY OF NEW YORK
BOROUGH OF MANHATTAN: FOURTH DISTRICT

WILLIAM FLOYD,
       Plaintiff

—against—

(Rev.) HARRY RIMMER and CENTRAL BAPTIST CHURCH OF NEW YORK, a corporation,

       Defendants

ANSWER

The Defendant, HARRY RIMMER, answering the Complaint of the Plaintiff herein, by his attorney, James E. Bennet, Esq., respectfully shows to the court and alleges:

FIRST: He admits that he is a preacher or evangelist and on the 1st day of November was a guest at the Hotel Wellington, New York City, but has no knowledge or information sufficient to form a belief as to the other allegations contained in paragraph marked "First" of plaintiff's Complaint and therefore denies the same.

SECOND: That he denies each and all the allegations contained in the paragraphs marked "Second," "Third," "Fourth" and "Fifth" of the plaintiff's Complaint, except that he received a letter dated November 1st, 1939, purporting to be signed by the plaintiff.

FOR A FIRST, SEPARATE AND DISTINCT DEFENSE TO ALL THE ALLEGATIONS CONTAINED IN THE SAID COMPLAINT, THE DEFENDANT RESPECTFULLY SHOWS TO THE COURT AND ALLEGES:

THIRD: That Defendant, Harry Rimmer, repeats and re-alleges each and every allegation contained in the above paragraphs "First" and "Second" of this Answer.

FOURTH: That the Defendant, Harry Rimmer, is a resident of the City of Duluth, State of Minnesota, and is also the President of the Research Science Bureau, a corporation located in Los Angeles, California. That the Research Science Bureau has made an offer as follows:

"The Research Science Bureau will pay $1,000.00 to any one who establishes a scientific error in the Bible, under the following conditions:

1. All applicants must state their case in writing, five duplicate copies of each thesis being submitted, so that each member of the Committee may have an identical copy for consideration.

2. Each thesis must be accompanied by the proof and evidence of the scientific error alleged.

3. The committee will not be obliged to attempt to harmonize scientific theories with interpretations

of the text; but will deal only with cases where an established fact of science is contradicted by a plain statement of the text.

4. The committee shall meet once each quarter and shall then answer all applicants who have submitted a claim in the preceding three months.

5. The decision of a majority of the committee shall be final in all cases."

which offer was read by the defendant at the meetings held by him in October and November 1939 in the Central Baptist Church, located at 92nd Street and Amsterdam Avenue, Borough of Manhattan, City of New York, and also over a radio broadcast conducted by that Church during such time, and that this offer is the only one which was mentioned by the said defendant, Harry Rimmer, at any time during his said preaching ministry in the State of New York, at the times referred to in the Complaint herein, and that defendant Rimmer at no time during said meetings did make any offer in his own behalf, or own name, and neither did he make any offer through the newspapers by printed notice or advertisement, or in any other way.

Fifth: That the plaintiff has not complied with the terms and conditions of the above offer in any way, manner or form, and that no award has been made by the Research Science Bureau, or any of its committee, for the payment of $1,000.00 or any other amount to the plaintiff herein in relation to his application mentioned in the said Complaint, or any other application of the plaintiff ever made at any time, and that there is therefore no amount due or owing from the said Research Science Bureau or the said defendant, Harry Rimmer, to the said plaintiff herein.

WHEREFORE, defendant, HARRY RIMMER, demands that the Complaint herein be dismissed together with the costs and disbursements of this action.

JAMES E. BENNET,
Attorney for the Defendant
Harry Rimmer
Office & P. O. Address,
38 Park Row
New York City.

Verified November 8th, 1939.

As you read the complaint, you doubtless noticed that no proof or evidence of any fact alleged accompanied the claim of MR. FLOYD, it was simply a statement of his own opinion in the matter. We find that these five contentions embodied in the complaint are typical of the case which infidelity always attempts to make against the Bible, and thus we are the more eager to show the fallacy involved in each of these spurious arguments. To get the matter in an orderly presentation, we will begin by citing from the Complaint, the following paragraph:

> "Four. That the specific errors in the Bible which the plaintiff specified and pointed out to defendant Rimmer in said letter of acceptance of his offer for a scientific error in the Bible, were in substance and effect the following, to wit:
>
> a) That the Bible states that the Creation was effected in six (6) days whereas the universe has evolved gradually through millions of years; as proven by many branches of science."

It will be noted that (1) no citation of the alleged proof is offered, merely a bare statement that "many branches of science" prove this "fact"; (2) and that the plaintiff has confused the *universe* and the *planet*. Any casual reader should note that the first chapter of Genesis connects the work of the six days only with the furnishing and tenancy of this single planet Earth. Also the specific statement that cosmic evolution has been *proved* will be a strange statement to all accredited scientists! It is not only in a highly theoretical stage at present, but is even less established than it was twenty years ago. The "fundamental law" of physics has done much to weaken the case for cosmic evolution.

To examine this charge, made in open court against the credibility of the Bible, we note that there are two issues involved. The first is the matter of origin. It must be recognized once and for all that there is no "science" of origin. Men of science, called scientists, may hold to individual theories concerning the beginning of things, but science itself does not and cannot deal with origin. A specific science is "a correlated body of absolute knowledge" concerning that particular subject, which knowledge has been derived by trained observers and demonstrated by experiment. How then, can there be a science of *origin?* Only philosophy or Revelation can speak in this field, and accredited scientists recognize this fact.

The second issue involved in this charge is the time factor as it applies to the age of the planet Earth, and to the length of the process of creation of that planet. The folly of claiming contradiction between

science and God's Word in this instance is clearly
seen when we note that there is no scientific proof
of the age of the earth, and there is no statement in
the Bible as to how long God was occupied in its
creation. This fact is consistently ignored by the
various classes of infidels.

The only statement that Moses makes as to the
length of the creation of the planet is in Genesis, the
first verse of chapter one: "In the beginning God created the heavens and the earth." In that statement no
slightest suggestion is made concerning the time involved in said creation. The second verse of Genesis
proceeds to the condition which prevailed before the
six-day period, and it is admittedly difficult to trans-
late from the Hebrew text into a completely idio-
matic English sentence. The best effort is probably
from Marlowe's translation, which states: "But the
earth had become empty; unfurnished: shrouded
with darkness and covered with water: and the spirit of the Elohim brooded over the face of the fluid
mass." The third verse then begins the presentation of a period of reconstruction during which God
furnished the earth for a new tenant, and crowned
the work of those six days with the creation of the
occupant. So we simply state that for the original
creative act which called the heavens and the earth
into being, no time limit is set or implied, and there
is no way of dogmatizing here. Nor can the research
of man, no matter how gifted he may be, establish
how long ago or how recently that act may have
occurred.

As to the statement that "many branches of science" have "proven" that the universe has been

evolving for many millions of years, that can only be classified as arrant nonsense. It is true that various scientists have advanced *theoretical* hypotheses as to the age of the earth, but their various attempts at demonstration have all signally failed as *proofs*.

It is commonly supposed by the unlearned, and also sometimes stated by deceivers who know better, that the "fossil record" proves the vast antiquity of the earth. The two sciences of geology and paleontology are appealed to here, and the stratographical record of historical geology is accepted as the basis of reckoning. First, certain "key" or "index" fossils are determined for each geological age, and a purely imaginary date is then given to each system of rock, according to these arbitrarily established fossils. The premise is that the simpler forms of life are always found in the *older rocks,* and the more complex orders of life are found in the younger rocks.

The folly of this system is seen first of all in the fact that the simplest forms of life that biology knows or has ever known, are still alive in our own day in unlimited numbers. We have kept them in our laboratories and studied them by the multiplied millions of billions, and that within the present century. *Every life form that makes up the fossil record of the Pacific Eocene is alive in the Pacific Ocean today, and that without deviation in form or substance.* Therefore the supposition that the simpler forms of life are the oldest, breaks down in the face of the fact that these so-called simple forms are all found in the twentieth century. I have spent much time in field study on this subject, and am prepared to show that there is no date system to be derived from the fossil record. The old exposé is still true, namely, "we date a rock system by the kind of fossils found in that rock; we date the fossils by the kind of rock in which we find them!"

2.   The second evidence of error here is the strange lack of unanimity on the part of the "experts." In the trial of this case, the star witness against the defendant was MR. WOOLSEY TELLER, vice-president of the A.A.A.A. This witness stated that the fossil record proved that the earth is two thousand million years old. But on cross-examination, MR. BENNET forced this witness to admit that the Harvard School holds to the figure of twenty million years, instead of two thousand million! That is quite a discrepancy for "science"! The witness further admitted that the opinion of the experts is far from unanimous, and that there will never be an authoritative agreement on the age of the earth. He stated that this matter can never be brought into court, to establish who is right and who is wrong! Thus the very "expert" whom the plaintiff depended upon to establish his case was forced to concede that there is no certain proof of the age of the planet to be derived from the fossil record; as the "guessiologists" differ between themselves by some one hundred and eighty million years!

The only other technique that scientists have advanced as a means of determining the age of the earth, is the hypothetical time it takes for radium to degenerate into lead. Not ALL lead is derived in this manner, but there is a specific type of lead which does result from the degeneration of radium. The theoretical process takes in five steps, and the theory

is well established by the work of such men as Dr.
Frederick Soddy, of the famous Thompson Laboratory, in London. The age of the earth, however,
has NOT been established by such means, and the
present conclusions that may be drawn from this
technique are very embarrassing to the world
of infidelity and evolution.

The "quantitative law" as applied to the degeneration of radium is easily stated: namely, one half
of a given mass deteriorates in a given time, and one
half of the remainder of the mass degenerates in the
same given time. As an instance, we may note that
a mass of *thorium x* will degenerate at the rate of
one half the original mass in four days. One half of
the remainder then degenerates in another four
days, and so on until the entire mass is dispersed.
ALL OF THESE STEPS ARE SURPRISINGLY
SHORT, and the antiquity phantom has been dis-
sipated by thorough research in this field. When
this law is applied to radium itself, the factor is two
thousand years. That is to say, it is presumed that
uranium will degenerate into radium at the rate of
one half the given mass in two thousand years, and
half of the remainder in another two thousand, and
so on to the end of the substance. And comparing
our known sources of uranium, pitchblende, etc., we
find that they could not have existed for more than
eight thousand years! This is quite different from
the wild guess of two billion years. And nine out of
ten of these guessers have never heard of this quantitative law.

To return to the complaint, which is the basis of
this court action, paragraph four then continues with

(b) That according to the first chapter of Genesis, the beasts were created before man; but according to the second chapter after man; neither occurred as there erroneously stated."

And there the plaintiff bit off another tremendous mouthful, which he did not even attempt to masticate when he had his day in court! There is nothing new or original in this allegation, as it is one of the stock arguments made very familiar by the ministry of Colonel Ingersoll in his day. It has been answered repeatedly, but the spirit of Antichrist which possesses the enemies of Christianity cares nothing for proof or reason. The simple allegation that creation did not occur as it is recorded in the Book of Genesis entitles us to ask the objector, in the language of the famous Baron, "Vas you there, Charlie?" In fact, this is just what MR. BENNET did ask the witness. His answer was obviously the only one he could make, he was not there. In that case, his assertion is hearsay, and has no weight in any forum which depends upon the laws of evidence.

The fact in the record is that there is no such conflict between the first two chapters of Genesis as modernism professes to find there. Let it be remembered that in the Hebrew text of the Old Testament, there is no first or second chapter of Genesis. The entire Book is one chapter, in the form in which Moses wrote the record. In what we commonly call the first chapter, Moses sets forth in a condensed form the entire sequence of God's work in the six-day period. Then, to clarify that account, he goes back and adds a few details to certain of those days and creative acts. These minor incidents he has passed over in the first account, in order that he might hasten on to an uninterrupted conclusion. In the additional data, he deals only with the work of two of the days, the third and the sixth.

And he is very careful not to get his order mixed, as the honest critic will be forced to admit, if he will consult the Hebrew text. The first statement of the "second chapter" is that Jehovah the Elohim made all the creatures of botany before any of them could grow, thus adding to the previous statement of the third day, for emphasis.

The next statement is "Then Jehovah the Elohim formed the man of the clay from the soil and breathed into his nostrils the breath of lives. And thus the man became a living soul."

Moses then reverts to the third day, but when he does he uses the past tense of the verb, and says, "And Jehovah the Elohim *had* planted a garden . . ." Thus also when the eighteenth verse speaks of the man, and the nineteenth verse goes back to the animals again, in order to keep the record accurate Moses states in the latter verse, "And Jehovah the Elohim *had* formed out of the soil every beast of the field . . ."

Any honest reader could refer to the Hebrew text and see this at a glance, or could read it thus in such a translation as Marlowe's "Book of Beginnings." This is a recognized principle in literature, and in any book but the Bible it would never even enter into a question of the truth of the contents of the book under discussion. But the vicious animosity against the Word of God, which is one of the paradoxes of this age, causes men who could and should be saved by this Book, to seek any occasion to discredit the Writing.

5.

ARGUMENTS AND REFUTATIONS

THIS fact was clearly demonstrated in the actual trial, when the plaintiff's witnesses sought to establish these allegations. As we will cover this in more detail in the following chapters, we merely present now a short summary of the arguments in the plaintiff's brief, or complaint, and offer the simple refutation which sets aside his fallacies. So we press on to the third item of Paragraph Four of the complaint, where the statement occurs:

" (c) That according to Genesis 6:19-22 Noah took two of every kind of living thing into the ark, whereas in 7:2-5 he took into said ark 'by sevens,' the male and his female; which allegations are not scientifically true, and said ark, as described in 6:14-16, could not possibly contain all such animals and living things and the food necessary for them during the long voyage."

Thus the plaintiff alleges that he knows more about the capacity and the load of the ark of Noah than the Designer or builder knew! When we consider that it was God who gave the instructions for the building of the ark, and that he specifically stated its dimensions, it is a little egotistical for some man to come along several thousand years later and claim

that he knows more about it than God did! Noah
found the boat satisfactory, the animals were all content there, and it is a little late to criticize the vessel
now.

Once more we are dealing with a criticism that is
hoary with antiquity, and which has been answered
times without number. This common citation of
error in the Bible is successfully refuted by two questions addressed to the objector. The first one is,
"What was the capacity of the ark?" Of course, the
difficulty is one that it is impossible to surmount, for
while the dimensions of the ark are given, its capacity is unknown. This is due to the fact that the length
of the antediluvian cubit is a matter of conjecture.
The earliest attempt to establish a standard cubit
was about 2200 B. C., perhaps a thousand years after
the date of the flood. Before that time, it might be
anything from the length of a man's forearm to his
complete height. Since the unit is thus variable, we
may know the dimensions of the boat, but not the
capacity.

The second question is, "How many different
species did Noah have to take into the ark?" Once
again we face a blank wall, so far as certainty is concerned. It must be remembered that true species
are comparatively few: varieties are infinite. Noah's
task was to load the ark with pairs of every true
species; seven pairs of the clean animals, and one
pair of the unclean. Since no accredited biologist
will ever hazard a guess as to how many species existed in the days of Noah, we have two variable factors, and no way to establish the value of either. In
a word, the critic is in the ridiculous position of one

who asserts that it is a scientific impossibility to get an unknown number of animals into an ark of unknown capacity! The results of this attempt will be reported later, when we come to the conduct of the actual trial.

The second objection in this allegation is equally fallacious. There is no contradiction between the two separate statements God made to Noah as to the cargo of the ark. His primary instruction was: "And of every living thing of all flesh, thou shalt bring a pair (two) of each kind into the ark to keep them with thee for the restoration of life; male and female shall they be." Thus was Noah instructed when the first order to build an ark was given to him (Gen. 6:19).

It is commonly believed that the work took 120 years. There is room for difference of opinion here, but certainly the work was not done in a day. But when the ark was ready, the Lord then instructed Noah in this detailed manner: "Enter thou and all thy house into the ark; for thee have I seen righteous before me in this generation. Of all the beasts that are clean, thou shalt take unto thee by seven and seven, the male and his female, and of the beasts that are not clean, one pair (two) of each, the male and his female. Likewise of the birds of the skies, seven and seven, male and female, to keep alive seed upon the face of all the land" (Gen. 7:1-3).

The apparent contradiction disappears when we see that God had first instructed Noah to take into the ark *pairs* of living things; of the unclean animals, one pair; of the clean creatures seven pairs of each species. The witnesses certainly failed dismally when they sought to convince the court that a discrepancy existed in this case.

The balance of Paragraph Four in the complaint was devoted to a monotonous repetition of some of the alleged zoological errors in the eleventh chapter of Leviticus. The same dreary ignorance that characterized Colonel Ingersoll's famous (or infamous) lecture, "The Mistakes of Moses," was once more made an issue in this suit. Specifically, the plaintiff charged scientific error against the Bible because in Leviticus 11:4-6 a list of unclean animals is given, and the Complaint charges: "It is stated that the camel does not divide the hoof and that the coney and the hare chew the cud, none of which statements is scientifically true, but the contrary is in every instance true."

It is difficult to comprehend how even an atheist can make such a colossal error as to maintain that the camel has a cloven hoof! All he had to do was to go out to the zoo and take a look. This simple procedure would have saved this plaintiff some later embarrassment. I presume he made the mistake by looking at the picture of a *skeleton* of a camel. In the osteological (bony) structure of the camel, there are only two toes on each foot that are developed. The second and third toe of the *Camelus Dromedarius* are well formed, but in the living creature they are enclosed in a cutaneous pad with a well-defined palmar surface, which forms a broad, elastic sole for the foot. Any person who has ever ridden a camel must have noted the foot of the beast when he mounted the saddle. If there is one place where zoology confirms Moses, it is in the matter of the camel's foot.

When the plaintiff had Rabbi Braunstein, who was his star witness, on the stand, the poor chap got all tangled up in his testimony, and didn't know whether he was supposed to testify that the camel reference was an error, because of the cud or because of the hoof! He stated that the camel did _not_ chew the cud (which it does) and that it did not divide the hoof, which the plaintiff claimed it did! This was one of the amusing incidents in the trial, and I quote briefly from the record at this point:

Plaintiff's Counsel: "According to Leviticus 11:4-6, it is stated that the camel cheweth the cud and does not divide the hoof, and that the coney and hare cheweth the cud. None of these statements is scientifically true, but the contrary is. Now, do you know if a camel divides the hoof?"

Defendant's Counsel: "I object. He is not a scientist, or zoologist."

Plaintiff's Counsel: "Anybody here who ever saw a camel can tell whether he chews the cud."

The Court: "Can they?"

Plaintiff's Counsel: "Yes."

The Court: "Say that again!"

Plaintiff's Counsel: "Why, yes."

The Court: "I venture to walk with you into a park, and we will see a hundred people there."

Plaintiff's Counsel: "And not one of the hundred will see a camel chewing the cud."

The Court: "I WILL BET YOU THEY WON'T KNOW!"

This argument between the judge and the attorney for the plaintiff lasted some time, to the amusement of the spectators, and finally the witness was again allowed to continue his testimony, in this fashion:

Plaintiff's Counsel: "Doctor, do you know whether the camel chews the cud or not?"

Answer: "Yes."

Question: "Does it, or does it not?"

Answer: "It does not."   (He was wrong!)

Question: "Is the camel cloven-hoofed?   Is the hoof divided, or is it solid like a horse?"

Answer: "My impression is that *it is solid*, like a horse."

The Court: "The doctor is guessing now, too!"

Plaintiff's Counsel: "HE GUESSED WRONG!"

You see, the plaintiff had put this witness on the stand to establish the "fact" that the camel has a cloven hoof, which it has not!   Instead the witness made a wild guess and, to the amusement of the court, he agreed with Moses.

Later, when the same witness was questioned about the "coney" and the "hare" the same difficulty arose.   The amusing episode began with a question by plaintiff's counsel:

Question: "Do you know about the coney and the hare, what kind of animals they are?"

Answer: "From a religious point of view they are unclean animals."

Defendant's Counsel: "I have the same objection. He does not know."

The Court: "He guessed at both of them. One he guessed right, and the other he guessed wrong!"

What a grand case they made against Moses! The presiding judge humorously charged the witness with *guessing*, and gave him a score of fifty per cent! Yet these same "guesses" have formed the framework of the case against the Bible for many generations. The *evidence* in the controversy is on the side of the believer, without a single known exception.

To return again to the Complaint, let us examine the case against Moses from the anatomy of these two disputed animals. The question at issue is, "Did the coney and hare of Moses' record chew the cud, or did they not?" Frankly, I do not know. The "hare" is an animal which is called in Hebrew text *arnabeth*, and nobody can identify it with any accuracy now. The word occurs only twice in the Old Testament, and both times in this eleventh chapter of Leviticus. It is variously translated in different versions, and it refers to an unknown animal. Certainly it is not the common *Lepus americanus*, or any other common variety of modern hare. Not even the "Easter bunny" which is reputed to lay candy eggs! The simple fact at issue is that Moses said *a certain unidentified animal chews the cud*: criticism says it did not!

The illustration of the coney is even more pertinent in establishing the weakness of the attempted demonstration against the accuracy of God's Word. Not only is this animal difficult to identify, but, if it is the one most commonly accepted by scholars, it has been extinct for two thousand years. The Hebrew text calls this creature the *shaphan*, and the Old Testament uses the word four times. The King James Version translates *shaphan* as coney; the Septuagint Version uses a Greek word compounded of two words for "pig," as if we were to say "swine-pig"; the American Revised Version translates it "coney," and in a note "rock-badger"; and the Douay Version uses the word "cherogrillus." Now you tell us what it is!

It is generally identified as a member of the order *Hyracoidea*, and most probably as the *Hyrax Syriacus*. The identification is not certain, but the few remains of this extinct creature make it the most probable of all the possibilities. The reader will concede that it is not possible to establish the digestive processes of an animal from its osteology (bone structure), and in fossil evidences we have few if any intestinal organs! A volume could be written about the odd paradoxes found in the Hyrax, and if it did not chew the cud it must have chewed gum!

The dentition (number, kind, and arrangement of teeth) would identify it among the rodents, except that the pulp is not active, as it is in the rabbits. The possession of two pairs of incisors in the inferior maxillary also shows that this cannot be any member of the rabbit family. Its front legs are long and the hind legs are short: just the reverse of all the rabbit order. The remains show four toes on the front feet and three on the rear feet, as in the tapir family. The toes are furnished with *nails* which closely resemble hoofs, and it may be identified with the ungulates (hoofed animals). But the exception is in the rear feet, where the inner toes have *claws*.

It sounds like a description of some weird beastie held over from the so-called Pleistocene period, or a visitor from Mars! With all these odd features it would be a wonder if this creature did not chew the cud! Of course I cannot say with authority, as I never saw one.

But Moses saw them in large numbers.

Who ought to know?

We offered to settle the argument this way: The "coney" has been extinct for 2,000 years. Mr. Floyd says they did not chew the cud, although he admittedly never saw one. Moses says they did; now let Mr. Floyd bring a coney into court and have him chew! If he does not have a cud, we will pay the one thousand dollars without further argument, upon this production of a living, non-cud-chewing *shaphan*. The offer was not accepted!

All of this has cleared the stage for the major opus of the infidels who met such a crushing defeat in this fresh assault upon the credibility of our Bible. The major portion of the Complaint dealt with an alleged mathematical demonstration of the "improbable" story of the visitation of the quail, and the entire case rested upon that charge. When the case was heard, this was to have been the final and crushing blow delivered against the Bible by the skilled witnesses who were to demolish its claims to infallibility, but at the end of the trial a strange thing happened. Discouraged by the complete collapse of every attempt to establish by legally acceptable evidence any of his other contentions against the Bible, the attorney for the plaintiff, MR. WHELESS, rested his case and withdrew from the battle, with no mention of the quail at all! Yet this was the major issue in the complaint, as you will observe by reading it again. And in every newspaper article and radio statement, this was the very heart of the controversy. To refresh the reader's mind, we quote again from the complaint:

"e) That in the Book of Exodus, said Bible, chapter 16, verse 13, it is stated: 'And it came to pass that at even the quails came up and covered the camp,' which same bare statement is elaborated and detailed specifications given in Numbers XI, 31-33:

31: And there went forth a wind from the Lord and brought quails from the sea and let them fall by the camp, as it were a day's journey on this side and as it were a day's journey on the other side, round about the camp, and as it were two cubits high upon the face of the earth.

32: And the people stood up all day and all that night, and all the next day, and they gathered up the quails: he that gathered least gathered ten homers; and they spread them all abroad for themselves round about the camp.

33: And while the flesh was yet between their teeth, ere it was chewed, the wrath of the Lord was kindled against the people, and the Lord smote the people with a very great plague."

In this citation we have omitted all of the attorney's comments, the cheap wit that seeks to ridicule God and His Word, and have just presented the essential facts. The brief then elaborates in eight sections the alleged errors in this record, and we condense it in this fashion:

6.

DISCUSSION OF ALLEGED ERRORS

Dɪꜱᴄᴜꜱꜱɪᴏɴ ᴏꜰ Aʟʟᴇɢᴇᴅ Eʀʀᴏʀꜱ:

1) Plaintiff alleges that a day's journey is 28 miles:

2) That a cubit is twenty-two inches:

3) That there was a square mass of quail surround ing the camp of Israel, piled up solidly on the earth to a depth of 44 inches, which mass was 2,992 square miles in area.

4) That there are 55 quail in a cubic foot:

5) That there were nineteen trillion, five hundred thirty-eight billion, four hundred sixty-seven million, three hundred fifty-six thousand, six hundred and seventy-two quail in the pile (19,538,467,356,672).

6) That each Israelite had to pick up and gather 85 quail per second.

It will be noted at once that there is a discrepancy between these figures and those in the suit prose cuted by this same attorney ten years ago. How start ling to find that what they swore to on oath ten years ago as being utterly scientific and accurate, is no longer so! Where would we have been if we had re jected the Word of God to suit their plea in 1929, on the basis of figures which were "scientific (?)" then, but are no longer so now? We would have been exactly where every other foolish person is who gives up the Word of God for human wisdom; namely, under the necessity of repenting our folly and returning to God's Book!

Ten years ago this same attorney pled that there were 4,569 square miles of quail; now he has only 2,992.

Ten years ago each Israelite had to pick up 97 quail per second, now it is 85.

Ten years ago there were 64 quail in a cubic foot, now there are only 55. Which has changed in size, the cubic foot, or the quail?

Ten years ago there were more than twenty-nine trillion quail in the mass or mess; now there are only nineteen trillion. What has happened to those ten thousand billion quail? Are we to believe that the children of Israel are still dining daily on the stock of quail, and that they have nibbled it down to this present figure?

Or, — fatal thought, — are we to consider that the plaintiff was mistaken ten years ago, and that maybe his figures were not "scientific" after all? In which case, is it not barely possible that he could be wrong again?

Indeed, it is not only possible; it is positive and certain that he is wrong! At least the court so decided, and the errors in his carefully constructed case are numerous and glaring.

In the first place, plaintiff cites an event that is recorded in Exodus 16, and adds to this record details of a second and separate event that appears in Numbers 11. A child should know better than this. The account of the first migration of quail, given in Exodus, occurred on the fifteenth day of the third month of the Exodus, while Israel was between Elim and Sinai. One month later, they reached Sinai and went into camp, where they stayed almost a full year. When they left Sinai they journeyed three days into the wilderness, and there ran into the second annual migration of quail, and suffered the experience that is recorded in Numbers 11. The details of this episode cannot be made to apply to the experience of the previous year, as the complaint alleges they do apply.

But the major fallacy is in three separate factors:

1) The shape and dimensions of the mass;
2) The length of a day's journey;
3) Whether the quail were piled up two cubits deep, or flying low.

The question has to do with the number of quail gathered by the Children of Israel, and to establish his claim of a gross error in the Bible, the plaintiff in this unusual action postulated that the quail were in a complete square, on all four sides of the camp. But the text specifically states that they were "as it were a day's journey from camp on this side, and as it were a day's journey on the other side." That is two sides only, and we cannot make a square with only two sides. The Hebrew text further states that these quail were a day's journey *from camp,* and does not say how wide the flight may have been. That is to say, that the quail coming in on an east wind, split their flight when they approached the camp, and passed it on the north and the south sides, about a day's journey away in either of these two directions. So the shape and dimensions of the flock are not as the plaintiff alleges.

The fantastic figures of the plaintiff are derived from the theory that a day's journey was 28 miles, and that the quail were thus piled up in an area 56 miles square. This figure is arrived at by assuming that they were twenty-eight miles to the north and an equal distance to the south, being 56 miles on that side. They are also alleged to have extended 56 miles east and west, and all calculations are then based on this supposition. No proof or evidence of the fact alleged is offered or even suggested, just the bare statement of a confessed enemy of the Bible that it was so. This fact must be kept in mind, as we are asked to reject the Word of God upon the unsupported word of one who offers no proof to justify his claim.

The fact of the matter is that a day's journey was just the distance that the Horde could cover in a given day, and it varied from day to day. The terrain covered had a lot to do with the mileage achieved, for one thing. At certain times they journeyed through deep sands, and progress was slow. At other times they were climbing rugged hills, or were pressing rapidly because water was scarce. But at no time did they make 28 miles in one single day. They carried all their camping equipment with them, and they pitched their camps before daylight failed. There were old men and women in the company, and above all else there were tender babes.

The Horde numbered about two and a half million people, and the minimum birth rate for such a number would be two hundred every day. Those new born babes must have slowed them down to some extent!

But most important of all, they had enormous flocks and herds. These animals all had to graze as they journeyed, and had to be watered as well. It is a matter of common knowledge that sheep are very tender, and cannot be driven far in one day. If sheep are being moved under emergency conditions, and there is urgent need for haste, they may be forced to make from eight to ten miles a day, for not more than three days. If they go longer than that, four to five miles is the absolute maximum for safety. This was a *long* journey, as it lasted 40 years! And the plaintiff in this case said they averaged 28 miles a day. In that case they were different from any sheep I ever saw, and they must have been crossed with antelopes!

This basic figure of 28 miles is purely a figment of the critic's own fevered imagination. Moses has given us part of the itinerary covered by the people in their wanderings, and we read this record in Numbers 33. The longest single day's journey they ever made was fifteen miles, and they rested for days to let their flocks recover. On two other occasions they made eleven miles in one day, and each time paused for days to rest the flocks again. Each of these instances was made necessary by shortage of water, and neither is to be taken as typical. On certain days they averaged from four to five and a half miles, and on many more they made from a mile and a half to three miles for the entire day. From Egypt to Sinai their flat average was three miles a day.

So even if the plaintiff was right, and the quail were in a solid square (which they were not) his figures are still fantastic and weird. For instance, if we square 56 and reduct the 144 miles of camp, as the plaintiff alleges must be done, we have 2,992 square miles of quail. But if we allow the maximum of five and a half miles a day, and square eleven miles, and deduct the 144 square miles of camp, we have 23 square miles less than no quail at all! Which is certainly *reductio ad absurdum!*

It being thus apparent that we cannot estimate the area, since we have no semblance of a defined region and no established unit by which to multiply, we scarcely need introduce the third point, which completely nullifies this attempted demonstration of error in the Scriptures. The issue turns finally on whether or not the quail were piled up two cubits deep on the face of the earth.

It is a fact that the King James Version of the Bible states "two cubits high *upon* the face of the earth." But this is a translation. The original language states that they were "two cubits *above* the face of the earth." This makes a world of difference.

In both the episodes of the quail, we are dealing with an annual migration which still goes on today. Every year the quail in northern Africa mass together in enormous flights, and migrate, as do ducks and geese in North America. They follow a traditional route on this flight, and the modern fowlers in Egypt hunt them even as was done in days of old. In nets and baskets they are captured; they are knocked down with long sticks; and many hungry folks get their most satisfactory meals in Egypt from this source. The surplus quail are dipped in hot salt water and dried or smoked, just as we do with ham or bacon in our national economy.

The quail has a very heavy body and small wings, and it does not fly high for long periods. They wait for a wind going their way in these long migrations, and thumb a ride part of the distance! At the end of a wind-driven flight, they are tired, and skimming along close to the ground. It is then that they fall easy victims to the hunters.

This is just what Moses was writing about. The annual flight passed near the camp, and the meat-hungry people went three or four miles from camp to gather them as they struggled past. But they were not *piled up* on the earth, and there is no possible way in which we could arrive at a "scientific" conclusion concerning the number that were gathered. It is conceded that the number must have been enormous. God had said that the Horde should have meat for thirty days, and there were two and a half million people to be fed by the quail that were gathered. It is not known how many hunters were active in the entire gathering, but the smallest number any one man gathered was "ten homers," or nearly 80 bushels. But the attempt to prove the exact number, down to one quail, is sheer folly, and violates all rules of intelligence.

It has often been noted that men who deny God and defy Him, do not submit to rules in any other sphere. Indeed, how can they? If a man has said in his heart, "There is no God," as a logical consequence he is supreme in his own right. This fact was emphasized in this suit in a striking manner. The attorney for the plaintiff, who is described in the magazine *Newsweek* as a noted Free-thinker. seemed to make up his rules as he went along! So it is fortunate that we have courts for such people.

Years ago all of the errors in his premise were pointed out to him, and he had a superb opportunity to correct his dangerous mistake. But instead he sought for another opportunity to drag the Bible into court, and assemble expert testimony to show that it is not, and cannot be, either inspired or credible. The witnesses came and were heard, the case was tried, and the plaintiff's case collapsed so pitifully that the court did not even suffer the defendants to make any reply! His ruling was arbitrary, since the law states that a defendant is neither obliged nor permitted to offer evidence until a case has been made against him, and there is no legal case to be made against the Bible.

Multiplied centuries of experience have taught men that there is nothing lax or loose about the presentation of evidence in a court of law, every attempt to prove an issue must be exact and specific. The law of evidence clearly states what may be offered and accepted in properly conducted trials, and what constitutes authority and proof. Therefore it is one thing to make broad statements concerning the alleged weaknesses of Holy Writ, but it is quite another thing to prove such contentions legally. For this reason, as well as for many others, the trial of the case of "FLOYD VS. RIMMER" attracted unusual attention, and was attended with close interest by many in all walks of life.

An editor of a famous New York newspaper asked for an interview when the suit was first filed, and after some hours of questioning he frankly stated, "Dr. Rimmer, every member of the staff of our large paper hopes that you will win this suit. We scarcely know a thing that is in the Bible, most of us have not read it for years, but we are unanimously *for* it. If that is gone, what do we have left?" This same spirit met us wherever the trial was discussed, and that was just about everywhere we went! It is true that the claims of God's enemies got most of the space in the publicity, when the case first started, but when the Scripture emerged from the test victorious, there was a note of satisfaction that was expressed even by those who make no pretention to faith.

The specific reason for the trial was that certain men hate the Word of God, and desired an opportunity to ridicule its contents and weaken its influence. The momentary occasion was an attempt to collect the reward of one thousand dollars for the proof of a scientific error in the Bible, without complying with the conditions of the offer. Attorney for the plaintiff knew that the attempt was utterly dishonest, as these conditions and terms of the said offer had never been met. Further, the letter demanding the award was followed within forty-eight hours with the filing of suit, thus allowing no time for the answer to have been given. Quite evidently none was expected or desired, as the suit was simply an excuse to propagate unbelief.

The court, however, could not consider this. It was only empowered to decide certain legal issues which were within its proper jurisdiction. There is no legally constituted body on this earth which has the power to decide whether the Bible is true or not. The writers of the Bible are all dead and have been so for many generations. Their testimony was undisputed in the days when they were alive and could be called into question, and while other witnesses to these same facts were also living. It is a fact recognized by the law of evidence that when the testimony of an eye-witness is not disputed in his own lifetime, that testimony is fixed for all time and is not subject to challenge by those who come after him. So the matter of the authenticity of the Bible is beyond the jurisdiction of any court.

The so-called science of each age is largely made up of the current *opinion* of men of science in that age. Their opinions and findings are subject to the discoveries and studies of later generations, and thus may be revised with the passing years. Indeed, they very generally are so revised. Very few of the scientific dogmatisms that I studied thirty years ago are still in vogue now. Therefore the most that can be brought to bear upon the question of the infallibility of the Bible is the general *opinion* of each age, and that is not acceptable legal evidence.

As an instance of what we mean, we may remind the reader that one of the specifications alleged against the Scripture was the statement; "The Bible states that the Creation was effected in six (6) days, whereas the Universe has evolved through millions of years . . ." We would like to know, right here and now, who is competent to testify here? The plaintiff alleged that we believe it all happened six thousand years ago, (which we do NOT believe) but that it was, in fact, two billion years ago. In either case, any living authority is too young to testify as to when it transpired!

7.

THE COURT GETS DOWN TO ESSENTIALS

S O THE court was limited to these considerations:

1) What offer was made?

2) Who made an offer?

3) Did the plaintiff, MR. FLOYD, comply with the terms of the offer?

4) Was an award made to him by Dr. Rimmer, and did the defendant refuse to pay the award so made?

On the thirtieth day of November, 1939, I submitted to an EXAMINATION BEFORE TRIAL in the office of my attorney, MR. JAMES BENNET, and at his advice and direction, I was, and am, perfectly willing to answer any and all legitimate questions. MR. BENNET very properly limited the questions to those that were within the issues of the suit. Instead of sticking to the stipulated issue, however, MR. WHELESS, the attorney for the plaintiff, attempted to conduct a glorified fishing expedition, insisting on conducting a snooping campaign into matters not mentioned in the complaint, and which he apparently hoped would provide material for a later suit. After repeated warnings by MR. BEN-

NET that if he did not stay within the issue we would leave the room and close the examination, he still persisted in his unethical tactics until we closed the matter by departing with counsel. But before that occurred, it had been established beyond question that the defendant was in total ignorance of the appearance of the public advertisement, was not a party to it, had authorized no person to insert such an offer, and was therefore not a party to any contract under the terms and conditions of said advertisement.

For this reason, judgment was rendered for the defendant.   Item one.

It was further established that THE RESEARCH SCIENCE BUREAU, INC., had made an offer, but that the offer was subject to five specific conditions. Therefore the proper party to appear as defendant in any such action would be the CORPORATION. This also made judgment for the defendant certain and legally imperative.   Item two.

The plaintiff, MR. FLOYD, did not comply with the terms of the offer, and therefore no award had ever been made to him. Thus judgment was rendered for the defendant. Items three and four.

But while the court was working toward this conclusion, the most amazing attempt against God's Word was going on in the court room. The judge allowed the plaintiff to call any accredited witness who could testify that there were scientific fallacies and errors in the Bible, and four men appeared to give their evidence against the Book that was written to offer mercy and grace to such as they and to us!

The trial was called and conducted in my absence, a circumstance which I shall ever regret. So I must depend upon the TRIAL RECORD for most of my information, and upon the report of my attorney and the friends who witnessed the trial. It seems strange to conduct a trial with the defendant absent, but I was away in another state, when the case was unexpectedly called. Rather than delay the action, the court vacated my subpoenas, which did not state either the time or the place, and therefore were not exactly legal and binding. However, with the case for the Bible in the very capable hands of ATTORNEY JAMES E. BENNET, and with my fortunes tied up to the Book, it was immaterial whether I was there or not!

The presiding judge was HON. BENJAMIN SHALLECK, with JUDGE SULLIVAN siting on the bench with him. The court gave the plaintiff every possible courtesy and advantage, sometimes to the seeming denial of the rights of the defendants. During the day and a half that the case lasted, MR. BENNET took numerous objections against the decisions of the judge, in order that his record might be kept straight in case of an appeal. But by this we intend no criticism of the Court or his conduct of the case. He was fair and just to both parties, as a capable judge should be.

The plaintiff had his choice of witnesses, and called four to the stand. His stated purpose was to prove by competent witnesses that there were scientific errors in the Bible, yet he did not produce one recognized scientist to testify to that fact!

This is highly important. The city of New York is recognized as a cultural center. The Rockefeller Institute is there, as well as the American Museum of National History, and the famous Metropolitan Museum. New York is the home of Columbia University and the College of the City of New York, as well as New York University. In any of these centers of culture and learning there are numerous accredited scientists; why did not one of them appear to testify to the fact that the Bible is in error on scientific subjects? Personally, I belong to several scientific associations, including one of more than twenty thousand members, The American Association for the Advancement of Science. In all of these groups I do not know of one accredited scientist who would take the stand to testify under oath that there are scientific fallacies in the Word of God!

The four witnesses were: a Jewish Rabbi of the "liberal" or modernistic Hebrew faith; a minister of humanism noted for his "liberal" tendencies; and another humanist minister who is an apostate from Unitarianism and an author of a book discrediting the Bible. Strange company: and rendered even stranger by the fourth witness, who is the vice-president of the American Association for the Advancement of Atheism. There is, of course, a strong mutual tie between these various schools of thought, consisting of their common scorn for the Holy Scriptures.

The first witness called to the stand was the Rabbi, Dr. Baruch Braunstein, who stated that he was in charge of the pulpit at the Congregation Beth Sholom, in the Bronx. He testified that he was a Doctor of Philosophy from Columbia University, and an authority on the text of the Old Testament. The witness did not get very far, and did the plaintiff no good whatever, in spite of the kindly attitude of the judge, who properly, because of the Rabbi's office, extended him every courtesy and consideration. In fact, there were times when the Court himself carried on a discussion with the witness, questioning his qualifications and his ability to testify as to the accuracy of the scientific portions of the Bible. As an instance of the weakness of the case when viewed in the light of legal procedure, we present this section from THE RECORD:—

Plaintiff's Counsel: "Are you familiar with the origins and authorship as disclosed by modern scientific criticism and searches, of the Book of Genesis, and the other five books attributed to Moses, the Pentateuch?"

Rabbi Braunstein: "I am, sir."

Question: "One of the propositions submitted here by the plaintiff to defendant Rimmer is that the Bible states that the creation was effected in six days, whereas the universe was created through millions of years, as proved by many branches of science. Now, if the Bible states in the first chapter of Genesis that the creation, the heavens and the earth and all the hosts thereof — were effected in six days, does that statement accord with modern scientific knowledge?"

The Court: "DON'T ANSWER THAT."

Defendant's Counsel: "Well, I certainly do object to that!"

The Court: "Objection sustained."

Plaintiff's Counsel: "Well, is it a scientific fact that the earth was created in six days?"

Defendant's Counsel: "I object to that."

The Court: "Objection sustained."

Plaintiff's Counsel: "I can show your Honor by one of Brother Rimmer's publications that he — that it is not a fact. He said that these — No, I am mistaken in that —"

The Court: "You have the Rabbi on the stand, and not Reverend Rimmer. So let us confine our questions to this witness and his qualifications and I will rule on whether he is properly qualified to answer the questions that you ask."

Plaintiff's Counsel: "May I ask whether your Honor is satisfied with his qualifications?"

The Court: "I don't know. It depends on what questions you intend to ask him. In the study of the Bible, yes; otherwise, no."

Plaintiff's Counsel: "As to his being a scientist?"

The Court: "Certainly I don't think he is a scientist, and I don't think the Doctor pretends to be a scientist."

Plaintiff's Counsel: "Certainly! nor am I, — but we all know a few things."

The Court: "THE MERE FACT THAT THE DOCTOR OR YOU MAY HAVE READ SOMETHING WHICH SAYS THAT THE SCIENTISTS DO NOT BELIEVE WHAT IS IN THE BIBLE, DOES NOT MAKE IT SO. You say that

Dr. Rimmer said that the creation was effected in six days?"

Plaintiff's Counsel: "Yes." (Note by Rimmer: "a deliberate prevarication!")

The Court: "You want to prove that this is a fallacy, that it is a scientific error?"

Plaintiff's Counsel: "Yes."

The Court: "PROVE IT . . . you want to prove by these many branches of science that the first statement in the Bible is not a fact. Now prove it."

Plaintiff's Counsel: "All right." Turning to the witness, he asked:

Q.: "Are you familiar with astronomy?"

A.: "I cannot pose as an authority on the science."

Q.: "Well, can you state definitely how long this universe has been in existence?"

Defendant's Counsel: "You certainly don't expect him to answer. If he does, I will object."

The Court: "He may say yes, or no."

The Witness: "Your Honor, I prefer, if I may, to make a statement."

The Court gave the required permission.

The Witness: "I would assume that I was asked to come here to state the position of the more or less liberal branch of the Jewish faith with respect to the Old Testament and the Bible. That I am prepared to do, and I feel, perhaps, you too may be qualified to do it. WHEN I AM ASKED TO MAKE REFER-

ENCES TO ASTRONOMY AND GEOLOGY AND PHYSICS, *I feel I have no right whatever.*" (Note by Rimmer: but the issue is over *scientific* errors, not *textual!*)

Then the Judge made this pertinent statement: "I am not concerned with Biblical criticisms in this case. I am concerned only with the fact that you allege that there is a scientific error in the Bible; that is, you are disproving the fact that there is no scientific error in the Bible. I am not concerned with criticism, therefore objection of Defendant's Counsel to this witness as a scientific witness is sustained."

Whereupon the Plaintiff's Counsel asked the Rabbi concerning his views of the accuracy of the text in general. The good Rabbi got hopelessly tangled up in a weird jumble of Wellhausen higher criticism, all of which has been discredited for almost a generation, and which is even more dead than Wellhausen himself! He tried to talk about the various manuscripts that make up a "composite Pentateuch." The "e," and the "J," and the "P," and after he struggled to a conclusion which had proved nothing:

Defendant's Counsel: "I MOVE TO STRIKE THAT OUT."

The Court: "WHY? I DON'T THINK IT DID YOUR CASE ANY HARM!"

Defendant's Counsel: "No, I don't think so either, but I want to keep my record straight!"

The next twenty-seven pages of THE RECORD are taken up with the direct examination of Rabbi Braunstein, and the arguments of the two Counsels, *and* the Court. At one stage of this argument, the Judge offered to bet Plaintiff's Counsel, MAJOR WHELESS, that he was wrong in his assertions! After which the Rabbi was excused from the stand without cross-examination, as he had not uttered a word that could count against the defendants. There was a general feeling that he was glad to be excused!

The second witness called in this attempt to discredit the Word of God was the REV. JOHN HAYNES HOLMES, who manifested a strange and eager willingness to testify under oath that the Bible is untrustworthy, and that it is contradicted by the facts of modern science. He did not have a happy time on the witness stand, to say the very least. Although he took oath upon his qualifications as a critic of the Scriptures, and declared under these solemn circumstances that he was qualified to speak on the scientific aspects of the case, he was later excused from testifying on everything that was pertinent to the issue, because he lacked the scientific ability necessary in such a witness. Asked if he was familiar with the sciences of astronomy, geology, archaeology and the other sciences that bear upon the question of the creation of the world, he replied, "Yes, quite familiar, as a fairly well educated man would be as to the knowledge of our times." With this modest assurance, the Plaintiff's Counsel proceeded to allow the witness to tell what he knew. The result was rather discouraging, as we see by THE RECORD.

Plaintiff's Counsel: "Referring to the statement in the first chapter of Genesis that the world was created in six days, and considering that it evolved through millions of years, what is the fact?"

Defendant's Counsel: "I object to that. The witness has not qualified."

The Court: "Objection sustained."

Plaintiff's Counsel: "Can you say it is scientifically true that the earth and the universe were created in six days?"

Defendant's Counsel: "I object to that, if Your Honor pleases."

The Court: "Objection sustained. If the doctor has made a study of that I will permit him to tell just what study he has made."

Plaintiff's Counsel: "Doctor, have you made any special studies that would sustain your allegations? And the conclusions of scientists?"

Ans.: "I know what the scientists think."

Counsel: "Now, is it scientifically true in accordance with—"

The Court, interrupting: "He is not using his own mind. He is using the mind of another scientist, and the objection must be sustained."

Counsel: "In your opinion, based on your scientific studies, is that six days—"

The Court, interrupting again: "You must first show the court what scientific studies he has made."

In the examination which followed, Dr. Holmes stated that his qualification as an expert on scientific subjects was based on the fact that he had read certain writers IN THE NINETEENTH CENTURY!

Not one man or authority of our century did he quote, or claim to be familiar with. Sic "modernism"! After a short and disappointing attempt to get his prejudiced opinions into the record, the witness was excused, with just one question for cross-examination. This question was asked and answered simply:

Question: "Dr. Holmes, do you believe that the Bible is the Word of God, the only infallible rule of faith and practice?"

Answer: "Of course not: certainly not!"

Whereupon Charles Francis Potter was next called to the witness stand, in an equally unsuccessful attempt to qualify him as a capable witness against the Word of God. He stated that he was a lecturer, and a writer of books, concerning the Bible. He further testified that he was an ordained Unitarian minister and had degrees qualifying him to teach ministers in theological seminary. He stated that he had studied and written on the various sciences, and had been an expert witness against God's Word in the famous trial at Dayton, Tennessee, when the defendant SCOPES was being tried for violation of the State law against teaching evolution as a fact in tax supported schools. As to *what* he was qualified to teach ministers, we will let THE RECORD of the trial show, in these words:

Question: "As far as you are concerned, the Bible is just a man-made book, full of man-made errors?"

Answer: "I have never seen any evidence of any other than human authorship of any book." (Query:

Does this include Dr. Potter's books denying the inspiration of the Bible?)

Question: "You never have had any connection with God in any way, have you?"

Answer: "I am not aware of having had any direct contact with God."

Question: "So far as you know, there is no God?"

Answer: "As I say, I am repeating what I have said before. I am an agnostic on the subject; God is the same as human individuals from my point of view."

Question: "That is your idea?"

Answer: "Yes, I believe that God is merely an idea of men's minds; that God was made in man's image, rather than that man was made in God's image."

But when it came to ability to demonstrate a scientific error in the Bible, the noted authority couldn't locate or prove one! He did assert that in testifying against the value of the Scriptures, he was giving the consensus of opinion of seventy-five scholars, but asked to name them or produce them he was unable to do so. Nonetheless, with amazing courtesy, The Court allowed him to state his opinions and conclusions for what they were worth. At the same time the Judge stated for the record that it would be impossible for the defendant to cross-examine these alleged seventy-five scholars, so the testimony might not be worth much. He was allowed to enter his denial of every historical fact connected with the flood, the ark and the creation. He said he had read a hundred books on the subject, but the only name he could remember among the authors was Darwin! When the witness left the stand, he had strongly impressed the court and all who had listened with the fact that he merely expressed the views of a certain school of thought, and that all of his "authorities" were of the same school! His presence did the case for inspiration no harm whatever, as under the skillful cross-examination to which he was subjected by MR. BENNET, he even denied the existence of God. It is to be expected that a man who believes God does not exist, would not believe that God had written a Book!

Before the next witness was called, the plaintiff's attorney, MR. WHELESS, made an unsuccessful attempt to tie the appearance of the advertisement in the *Herald-Tribune,* upon which the suit was based, to the defendant, HARRY RIMMER. The court refused to hold the defendant responsible, as the means of connection proved to be a farce. MR. WHELESS contended that the defendant had made a personal offer in 1927 of one hundred dollars to the discoverer of a scientific error in the Bible. Therefore the notice of a thousand dollars, put in the *Herald-Tribune* must have been by the same party, as they are practically identical! The court ruled that since there was no proof offered of continuance between 1927 and 1939, the case was not established. JUDGE SHALLECK further stated that if he himself had put an advertisement in the paper without my knowledge, even though he used my name, it would not be binding upon me. Therefore the only hope of the plaintiff was to establish a prima facie case against the Bible, and this they proceeded to try to do.

MR. WOOLSEY TELLER, being called to the stand, identified himself as an editor, a scientific writer, and a scientific lecturer. In attempting to qualify, he praised himself so highly that the Judge interrupted the witness to say to him, "DON'T LET YOUR EGO RUN AWAY WITH YOU!" The personal interest of this witness in the case may be judged from the fact that he is a vice-president of the AMERICAN ASSOCIATION FOR THE ADVANCEMENT OF ATHEISM. One would scarcely expect the Word of God to receive very kindly and honest consideration from such a source!

The witness stated that he had no degrees or recognized standing, but that he was a self-educated man. His knowledge of science was purely a reading knowledge, as he had never been with an expedition, done laboratory research, or conducted original investigation into source material in any branch of science. Like many another so-called "authority" who influences the public by means of the printed page, this gentleman is engaged in the lucrative project of purveying second-hand opinions on matters of general public interest. How wrong he was may be demonstrated in the fact that MR. TELLER still clings with a child-like credulity to the exploded myth that the human embryo has a tail, which he described as being "longer than the hind legs of the individual!" He extended his remarks to state that certain adult individuals were known to possess fully developed tails, and one such had been photographed by Dr. Keen.

We did not think that such sublime and contented
ignorance could exist, even in an atheist! Had he
taken pains to learn anything in the last twenty-five
years, MR. TELLER would have known that Dr.
Keen had been made the victim of a hoax. An enter-
prising photographer in Manila took a picture of a
naked Igorrote, and then retouched his plate, draw-
ing in a tail. This he sold to the soldiers and tourists
in the Philippines, partly as a joke. One of Dr.
Keen's grandsons was a doctor with the Medical
Corps of the U.S. Army, and he got one of these pic-
tures. Knowing his grandfather's interest in evolution, he sent the old gentleman one just in the spirit
of fun.

But the elder Dr. Keen received the picture as
manna from Heaven! You know that the theory of
evolution is so decrepit, and feeble, that even a rub-
ber crutch is more than welcome. So in his famous
book: "I BELIEVE IN GOD AND EVOLUTION"
Dr. Keen reproduced this faked picture as an evidence of animal origin for man. DR. WILLIAM
BELL RILEY exposed the fraud, and DR. KEEN's
grandson came forward and admitted that it had all
been intended as a joke. Whereupon DR. KEEN
withdrew the entire issue or edition of his book, and
reprinted it without the tale of the tail! But the eminent, self-qualified MR. TELLER still swallows the
Igorrote, tail and all.

On the matters dealing with science, this witness was equally vague, and manifested the same sad
ignorance. It is time that science revolted against
the common custom of being used as a mask to hide
the face of the old hag Atheism; enough burdens

are borne by the world of research without this added onus. To show the pitiful plight of one who labors against God's Word under the rigid requirements of the law of evidence, let us again refer to THE RECORD:

Plaintiff's Counsel: "Now, what is the age of the earth?"

Mr. Teller: "You want my opinion? Or the consensus of opinion?"

Plaintiff's Counsel: "The consensus of opinion."

Mr. Teller: "Roughly speaking, about two thousand million years."

The Court: "IS THAT A GUESS?"

Mr. Teller: "No, sir, that is formulated from the release of radio-activities that go on, and also from geological strata."

The Court: "On what do you base your conclusions?"

Mr. Teller: "The concensus of scientific opinion." When the Court and both Counsels pressed this man for the authorities upon which he based his statement, he could only recall three names. These were two very popular writers of light books for the general public, Sir James Jeans and Dr. Eddington, whose initials the witness did not know; and Dr. Schuchard of Yale University. YET THE WITNESS STATED UNDER OATH THAT THERE WERE ABOUT TWO THOUSAND SCIENTISTS who should be heard on this subject. And then he accepts the popular opinion of just three men as the "consensus" of scientific thought on the matter, and seeks to reject the Genesis account of creation upon the authority of three fallible human beings, who will be forgotten within a century of their deaths!

To complete the pitiful display of the mental limitations of atheism, when asked to account for the origin of the earth on some other basis than that of specific creation, the witness took refuge in the out-moded nebular hypothesis of LaPlace, with some possible recent corrections. He stated the ancient theory that two stars were passing each other, and one star pulled loose a mass of the other, which mass began to revolve, thus forming the earth. And right here I would like to interpolate a comment. Every school-boy knows of the cohesion inherent in bodies of matter, and the amount of power essential to break up such a mass. If two stars passed each other, and one had sufficient power of attraction to pull part of the other mass loose from the parent body, THE LOOSE MASS WOULD SMACK RIGHT INTO THAT POWER SOURCE AND CLEAVE TO IT. Thus, instead of creating an independent third body, the stronger body would be enlarged by the addition of the mass it had attracted. If you have access to a laboratory, demonstrate this with an electro-magnet!

To return to the witness, he was asked where these stars came from.

He replied that they were nebulae that had condensed.

Asked where the nebulae came from, he said it was condensed ether.

AND THE ETHER, HE SAID, WAS ALWAYS THERE!

If we have to start with something, and cannot account for the origin of that original matter, *why not start with God?* After reading the record of this interesting failure of skepticism to make any case against the Bible, we are praising God with renewed joy that we have at least the minimum sense required to realize that "the heavens declare the glory of God, and the firmament showeth the work of His fingers." Yet this poor befuddled witness admitted on the stand that every thing in the world that functions had a maker, EXCEPT THE WORLD ITSELF!

All of this testimony was introduced into the record by the skillful cross-examinations of the atheist by MR. BENNET, who forced the witness also to admit that there are learned men in denominational colleges who believe the Bible to be the Word of God. THE RECORD contains such illuminating passages as this, in the cross-examination of MR. TELLER.

Mr. Bennet: "There are learned men . . . professors of anthropology, embryology, cosmology and all these other sciences . . . who do not look upon the Bible with scorn?"

Mr. Teller: "They can't afford to. It's their job."

Question: "They accept the Bible as the Word of God, as far as you know?"

Answer: "Yes."

Question: "As a Book to be honored, respected and believed?"

Ans.: "Yes."

Question: "There are a great many of them, are there not?"

Ans.: "Yes."

Question: "As far as you know, they treat the Bible with respect?"

Ans.: "Yes."

Question: "Do you believe in God?"

Ans.: "No, sir!"

Plaintiff's Counsel: "I object, if your Honor please, and ask that that answer be stricken out. That is a perfectly impertinent question."

The Court: "Overruled."

Mr. Bennet: "All this testimony is given from the standpoint of a man who does not believe there is a God!"

The Witness, MR. TELLER: "My evidence is given from the viewpoint of what I have been able to learn from science, which has brought me to the conclusion that there is no God."

There are several noteworthy facts to be weighed in that passage, and it would take many volumes the size of this one to follow them all to their final conclusions. First, there is the admitted fact that to believe the Bible is not necessarily a mark of inferior mentality! MANY learned men are confessed by the atheist to hold reverence for the Word of God; maybe we have not been so dumb after all in believing what God has revealed! The second point is that an atheist considers it "impertinent" to ask him if he believes in God! No Christian is ashamed to answer such a question, nor hesitates to confess his faith in the Most High. Why should a man hold a private belief that he is reluctant to admit in public? Devious indeed are even the mental ways of darkness.

But the most important of all is the very apparent falsehood in the statement of this witness that his studies of science convinced him there is no God. The fact of the matter is, that believing as an atheist, he studied certain biased viewpoints to *bolster his belief* that God does not exist! All of his scientific thinking is shadowed by the preconceived conclusion with which he approaches his studies, and science has no place in his thinking. Dogmatic conclusions are first erected, and then poor, long-suffering science is asked to sustain the ignorance of a darkened heart and mind.

8.

THE TRIUMPH OF THE BIBLE IN A
NEW YORK COURT

THUS there was no other course open to the court than to bring judgment for the defendants, which he finally did. In the most emphatic terms he could use, HON. JUSTICE BENJAMIN SHALLECK ruled that the defendants had not inserted the advertisement in the *Herald-Tribune* on which suit was based, and therefore no contract existed:

The defendant RIMMER *had* made an offer in the name of and for the corporation, but that the conditions of said offer had not been met:

And that the PLAINTIFF had failed to make a prima facie case against the Bible, and therefore the defendant would not even be permitted to testify! The judge reminded the PLAINTIFF that the DEFENDANT was not expected or entitled to answer until something had been proved against him, and said, sternly, "YOU HAVE WASTED THE TIME OF THIS COURT FOR A DAY AND A HALF, AND YOU HAVE FAILED TO PROVE ONE SINGLE ITEM!" Therefore judgment was rendered for the DEFENDANTS, and the court of New York has again decided that *it is all right for Christians to go right on reading and believing the Bible!*

I do not claim to be able to answer any and every question that can be asked about difficulties in the Bible, but I *do* maintain that given time enough an answer can be *found* to any problem and difficulty that reason can raise in the reading of God's Word. For twenty-seven years I have been engaged in the study of the sciences that touch upon the content of the Bible, and I have never yet found an error in its marvelous pages. I stand ready to produce, or to find the answer to every argument of infidelity, for those years have taught me that "holy men spake as they were moved by the Spirit of God" and their words are without error or fallacy.

The Plaintiff in this case filed a list of 53 alleged scientific errors in the Bible, and every single one of them was revived and revamped from the ancient display of ignorance indulged in by the late Col. Ingersoll. This is not surprising, as there is no originality in atheism. But almost any one of the 53 could be answered by the average Sunday School scholar past the age of twelve!

The Plaintiff offered to withdraw his suit if I would admit that these errors existed. I simply replied that I would rot in jail a thousand years for each of his 53 points, before I would confess to a lie like that! In the face of this court decision, we bless God, take new courage, and press on.

2199

28^f Gen 1-2, 6

: 16 Quail acct

37 Gen 1: 31 — has to
do nls w/ evltt

38 & Gen 1: 2 Transl.

45f. Gen 6f

48 Lev 11: 4-6

62 on th Quail